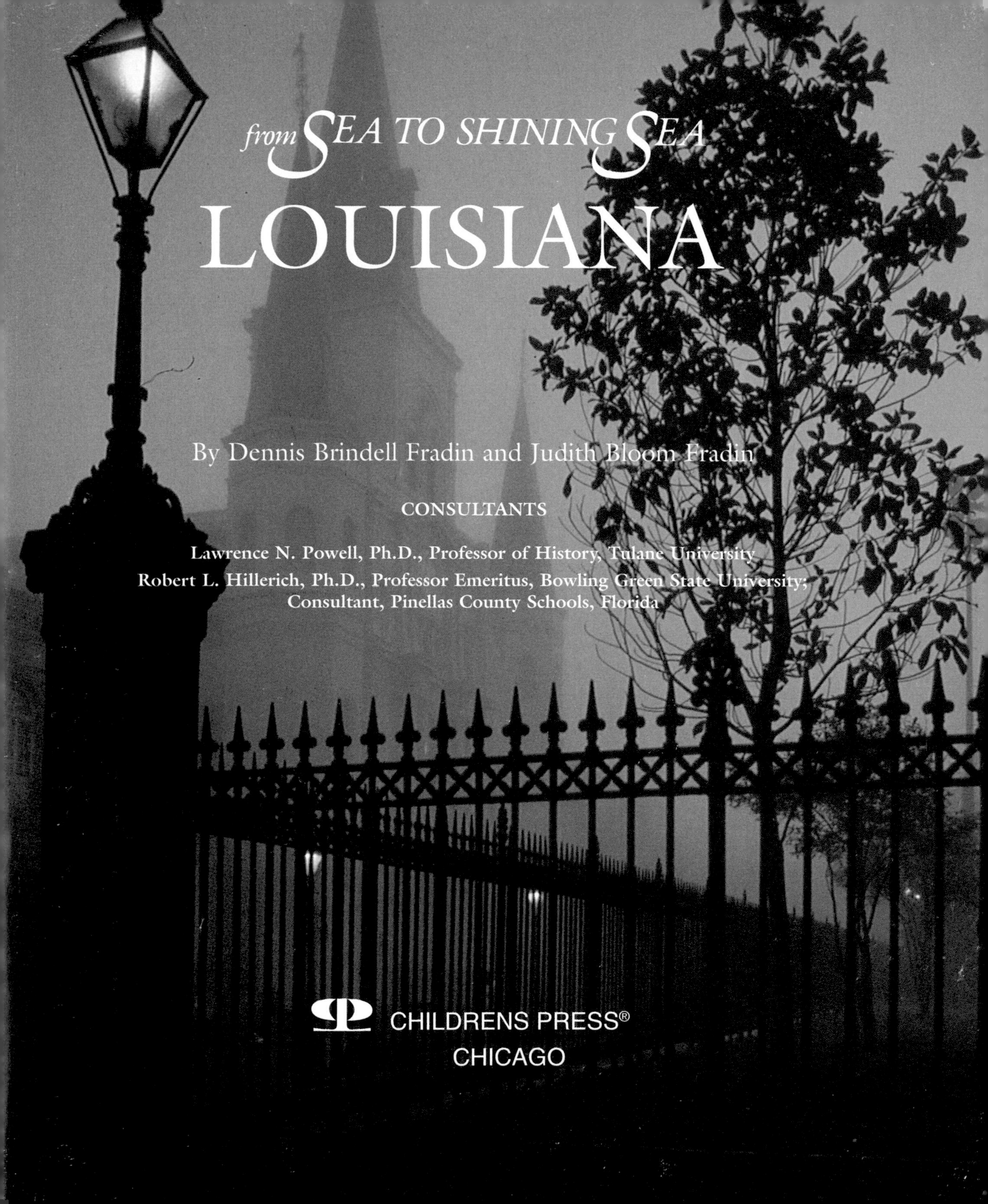

from SEA TO SHINING SEA

LOUISIANA

By Dennis Brindell Fradin and Judith Bloom Fradin

CONSULTANTS

Lawrence N. Powell, Ph.D., Professor of History, Tulane University

Robert L. Hillerich, Ph.D., Professor Emeritus, Bowling Green State University;
Consultant, Pinellas County Schools, Florida

CHILDRENS PRESS®
CHICAGO

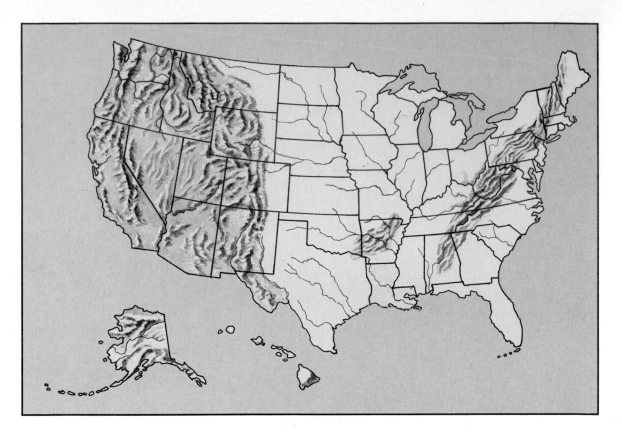

Louisiana is one of the fourteen states in the region called the South. The other southern states are Alabama, Arkansas, Delaware, Florida, Georgia, Kentucky, Maryland, Mississippi, North Carolina, South Carolina, Tennessee, Virginia, and West Virginia.

For our cousin Kathie Brindell, with love

Front cover picture: Oak Alley Plantation, Vacherie; page 1: Morning fog, Jackson Square, New Orleans; back cover: Gravenburg Swamp, Atchafalaya Basin

Project Editor: Joan Downing
Design Director: Karen Kohn
Typesetting: Graphic Connections, Inc.
Engraving: Liberty Photoengraving

Library of Congress Cataloging-in-Publication Data

Fradin, Dennis B.
　Louisiana / by Dennis Brindell Fradin & Judith Bloom
Fradin.
　　p.　cm. — (From sea to shining sea)
　Includes index.
　ISBN 0-516-03818-4
　1. Louisiana—Juvenile literature.　I. Fradin, Judith
Bloom.　II. Title.　III. Series: Fradin, Dennis B.
From sea to shining sea.
F369.3.F68　1995　　　　　　　　　　94-37566
976.3—dc20　　　　　　　　　　　　　　CIP
　　　　　　　　　　　　　　　　　　　　AC

Table of Contents

*Costumed people in
the New Orleans
Mardi Gras Parade*

INTRODUCING THE PELICAN STATE

Louisiana was named by explorer René-Robert Cavelier, Sieur de La Salle, in honor of King Louis XIV of France.

Louisiana is a southern state on the Gulf of Mexico. Long ago, many brown pelicans lived along Louisiana's coast. One of Louisiana's nicknames is the "Pelican State."

Louisiana is a blend of many people. Another of its nicknames is the "Creole State." Creoles are descendants of Louisiana's first French and Spanish settlers. Louisiana's descendants of French people who came from Canada are called Cajuns. The state also has one of the country's highest percentages of African Americans. The food and music of all these people bring many visitors to Louisiana.

Today, Louisiana leads the country at producing shrimp, crawfish, and salt. Louisiana is also a giant oil and natural-gas producer.

Much more is special about Louisiana. Where is the world's longest bridge? Where is the country's most famous Mardi Gras festival held? Where were trumpeter Louis Armstrong and playwright Lillian Hellman born? Where was the rocket made that launched the first astronauts to the moon? The answer to these questions is the Pelican State: Louisiana.

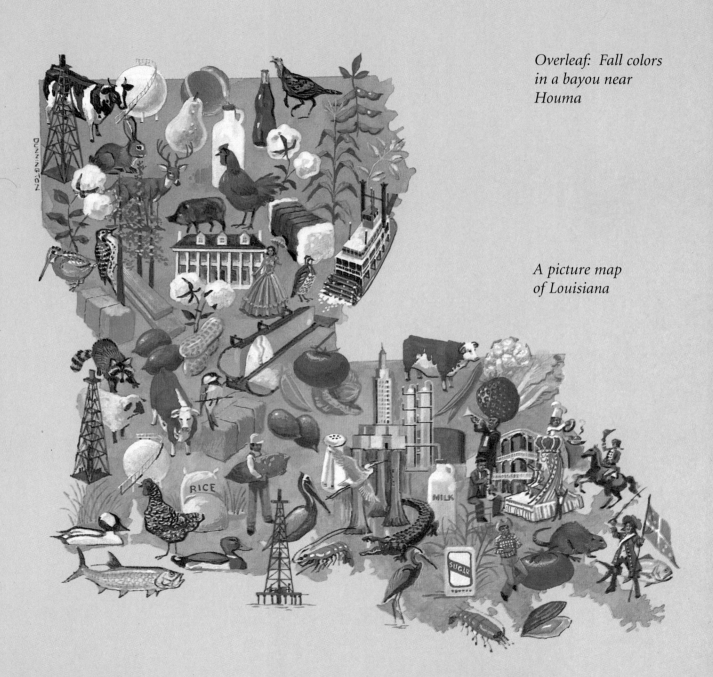

Overleaf: Fall colors in a bayou near Houma

A picture map of Louisiana

Bayous, Magnolias, and Alligators

Bayous, Magnolias, and Alligators

Louisiana is a boot-shaped state in the South. It covers nearly 48,000 square miles of land and water. Mississippi is east of Louisiana. Arkansas is to the north. Texas is to the west. The Gulf of Mexico lies to the south and east.

All of Louisiana is made of low-lying plains. That is why Driskill Mountain is the state's highest point. It is only 535 feet above sea level. The lowest point is 5 feet below sea level. That is at New Orleans. The plains have rich soil to farm. Under the land lie oil, gas, and salt.

Water, Woods, and Wildlife

Water hyacinths and lotus blossoms in the Atchafalaya Basin

Louisiana is one of the most watery states. Nearly one-third of Louisiana is wetland. Many marshes and swamps lie near Louisiana's coast. Lakes and ponds also dot the state. Lake Pontchartrain is Louisiana's largest lake. It covers 625 square miles north of New Orleans. This lake is partly saltwater.

The country's longest river ends its journey south of New Orleans. There, the Mississippi River empties into the Gulf of Mexico. The Red, Black,

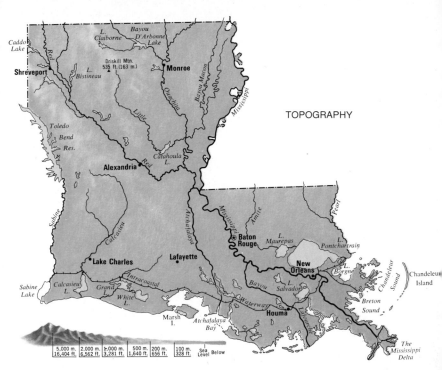

TOPOGRAPHY

Calcasieu, Sabine, and Pearl are other Louisiana rivers. Louisiana also has many bayous, such as Bayou Teche and Bayou Lafourche. These are shallow, slow-moving, riverlike waters. They are formed from the overflow of lakes and rivers.

Louisiana is one-half wooded. The bald cypress is the state tree. It grows in Louisiana's wetlands. Oak, magnolia, pine, and sweet gum trees also grow in the state. Spanish moss hangs like beards from bald cypress and oak trees. The magnolia tree's blossom is the state flower. Azaleas, camellias, and jasmine add to Louisiana's garden of sweet southern smells.

Left: Bald cypress, the state tree

9

Louisiana's wetlands are home to alligators, otters, and nutrias. Nutrias look a little like beavers. Deer, bobcats, and raccoons live in the woods. Sea turtles and dolphins can be seen along the Gulf of Mexico. The brown pelican is the state bird. Louisiana is the winter home for millions of ducks and geese. Woodpeckers, swans, herons, and owls also fly about Louisiana. Fish in the state include bass and catfish. Shrimp, oysters, and crawfish are Louisiana shellfish.

Left: A nutria
Right: A great egret with her young

CLIMATE

The Atchafalaya Swamp

Louisiana has a hot, wet climate. Summer temperatures often top 90 degrees Fahrenheit. Winter temperatures often hit 60 degrees Fahrenheit. Louisiana averages 57 inches of rain a year. That makes it the rainiest state. Heavy rains sometimes cause Louisiana's rivers to flood.

Hurricanes sometimes hit Louisiana's coast. These giant windstorms start over the ocean. In 1957, Hurricane Audrey killed more than 350 people in Louisiana. Hurricane Andrew hit Louisiana in 1992. Winds up to 140 miles per hour battered the coast.

From Ancient Times Until Today

FROM ANCIENT TIMES UNTIL TODAY

Millions of years ago, seas covered Louisiana. Fossils of a whale's bones have been found in central Louisiana. Bones of ancient elephants and small horses have also been uncovered.

Opposite: A 1925 picture of workers at the Roseland Veneer and Package Company

AMERICAN INDIANS

People reached Louisiana at least 12,000 years ago. Almost 4,000 years ago, ancestors of today's Indians began a village. Mounds from the village remain northeast of Monroe at Poverty Point. About 1,000 years ago, other mounds were built near Marksville. Beautiful pottery was found there.

By the 1500s, about thirty American Indian groups lived in Louisiana. The Caddo, Houma, Tunica, Attakapa, and Chitimacha were among them.

A Marksville burial mound

EUROPEAN EXPLORERS AND SETTLERS

In 1541, Hernando de Soto discovered the Mississippi River. He crossed from present-day

René-Robert Cavelier, Sieur de La Salle (center), claimed the Mississippi Valley for France on April 9, 1682.

French Louisiana reached from the present-day state all the way to Montana.

Mississippi into Louisiana. De Soto died near what is now Ferriday, Louisiana, in 1542.

French explorer La Salle traveled down the Mississippi River in 1682. On April 9, he arrived at the river's mouth. That is where it empties into the Gulf of Mexico. La Salle claimed the whole Mississippi Valley for France. He named the region Louisiana for his king, Louis XIV of France.

In the early 1700s, the French began settling what is now Louisiana. Natchitoches was the first settlement. Louis Juchereau de St. Denis began it in

1714. In 1718, Jean Baptiste Le Moyne began New Orleans. In 1722, New Orleans became French Louisiana's capital.

Some French people built plantations in Louisiana. They grew tobacco and indigo on these large farms. The French brought in black slaves from Africa to do the work. By 1763, Louisiana's population was about 7,500. Nearly half were slaves.

A year earlier, France had given Louisiana to Spain. A few Spaniards moved to Louisiana. The Spaniards brought in more black slaves. There were many "free people of color" in Louisiana. From the 1760s to the 1790s, about 4,000 Acadians came to Louisiana. These were French people from Canada. The British had driven them from their homes. Their descendants are called Cajuns.

THE UNITED STATES BUYS LOUISIANA

By 1783, the United States owned most land east of the Mississippi River. Some American trappers, traders, and settlers crossed the river. In 1800, Spain returned Louisiana to France. Three years later, the United States bought Louisiana from France. The Louisiana Purchase cost $15 million. Most of what

This statue of La Salle in Kenner marks the spot where he landed and claimed land for France.

The parts of Louisiana that the United States did not obtain from France in 1803 were obtained from Spain in 1810 and 1819.

15

is now the state of Louisiana was included. So was all or part of fourteen other states.

Many Americans moved to Louisiana. Most of them came from the southern states. By 1810, Louisiana had 76,556 people. That was enough for statehood. On April 30, 1812, Louisiana entered the Union. It became the eighteenth state.

In January 1812, the *New Orleans* traveled down the Mississippi River. It was the first steamboat to reach New Orleans. People began traveling the river by steamboat. These vessels also carried grain, cotton, and sugarcane to New Orleans. The city became an important trading center.

Later in 1812, war broke out between the United States and England. The War of 1812 (1812-1815) was fought over trade and sea power. On January 8, 1815, the English tried to capture New Orleans. General Andrew Jackson led a group of volunteers. They included soldiers, Indians, free black people, and even pirates. The Battle of New Orleans was a great American victory.

Jean Lafitte was the most famous of the pirates. He and his men controlled Barataria Bay.

THE CIVIL WAR AND RECONSTRUCTION

Louisiana also had about 19,000 free people of color by 1860.

By 1860, more than 330,000 of Louisiana's 708,000 people were black slaves. Louisiana's planters used slaves to grow and harvest cotton and sugarcane. Slavery was no longer allowed in the North. In November 1860, Abraham Lincoln was elected president of the United States. He was a northerner. Southern leaders feared that he would outlaw slavery in the South, too. Eleven southern states seceded from the Union. Louisiana seceded on January 26, 1861. Those eleven states set themselves up as a separate country. They called it the Confederate States of America.

On April 12, 1861, the Civil War began. Pierre Beauregard of New Orleans was a Confederate gen-

General Andrew Jackson's victory at the Battle of New Orleans in 1815

*Confederate General
Pierre Beauregard*

*Pinckney Pinchback,
governor of Louisiana*

eral. He ordered the war's first shots. That happened in South Carolina. Louisiana provided about 56,000 Confederate troops. For four years, the Confederacy (South) fought the Union (North). Some southerners remained loyal to the Union. Captain David Farragut was a Tennessean who had lived in Louisiana. In April 1862, Farragut's Union fleet captured New Orleans. The Union then controlled the Mississippi River.

The war ended in April 1865. The South surrendered. In December 1865, the United States government freed all the slaves. But the southern states weren't allowed back in the Union right away. They had to form new governments. They had to pass laws to protect the rights of black people. This was called Reconstruction. On June 25, 1868, Louisiana became part of the United States again. But United States troops remained until 1877. They made sure that blacks were allowed their voting rights. Pinckney Pinchback became the country's first black state governor (1872-1873).

CHANGES IN FARMING, INDUSTRY, AND PEOPLE

After the Civil War, many Louisiana cotton growers became sharecroppers and tenant farmers. Both groups farmed other people's land and were usually poor. Sharecroppers had to give part of their crops to the landowners. Tenant farmers had to pay rent for using their land. In the 1880s, irrigation made it possible for rice to become a big Louisiana crop.

Meanwhile, lumber and flour mills were begun. Railroads were built. They linked Louisiana with the rest of the country. The Mississippi River's mouth was deepened. This made New Orleans a good port for oceangoing ships. Oil was found near Jennings in 1901. It was used to make gasoline for automobiles. Natural gas was found near Monroe in 1916. It was needed to cook food and heat homes. All this growth attracted more people. By 1900, Louisiana's population was 1,381,625. It had almost doubled since the Civil War.

Life for Louisiana's black people had become worse. The vote was taken from Louisiana blacks in 1898. Segregation took root throughout the South. There were separate schools for blacks and for whites. Black people could not mix with white people on buses or in restaurants. Some black people fought the unfair laws. The Ku Klux Klan and other hate groups attacked them. Between 1882 and 1935, about 350 black Louisianans were lynched. They were hanged by mobs without a trial.

Sharecroppers bringing a bale of cotton to market

WORLD WARS, DEPRESSION, AND CIVIL RIGHTS

Huey Long

In 1917, the United States entered World War I (1914-1918). About 75,000 Louisianans helped win the war. Many Louisiana doctors and nurses cared for the wounded in France and Italy.

The Great Depression (1929-1939) brought hard times to the whole country. Banks and factories closed. Workers lost their jobs. Farmers lost their land. Huey Long governed Louisiana from 1928 to 1932. Under Governor Long, many Louisianans got jobs building roads and bridges. He passed out free textbooks. That helped poor children attend school. Then Long served in the United States Senate (1932-1935). Senator Long began the Share-the-Wealth Society. It promised every American a base income. But Huey Long made many enemies. One of them shot him in 1935. Long died of his wounds.

In 1939, Huey Long's youngest brother became Louisiana's governor. Earl Long served three terms as governor (1939-1940, 1948-1952, and 1956-1960). He, too, worked to improve education. Earl Long also tried to make life better for black people.

In 1941, the United States entered World War

II (1939-1945). Many ships were built in New Orleans for the United States Navy. Nearly 300,000 Louisiana men and women served their country.

After World War II, Louisiana farmers began to plant soybeans. They soon passed all other crops grown in the state.

In the 1950s, black people began to win back their rights. In 1958, segregation on New Orleans buses ended. Black children and white children attended the same schools in 1960. Segregation also ended in other public places. Blacks throughout the

Wooden boats made in this New Orleans factory carried American troops ashore in Sicily and Italy during World War II.

21

South won their voting rights. Once more, blacks were elected to office. In 1977, Ernest N. Morial was elected the first black mayor of New Orleans.

RECENT TIMES

Louisiana helped begin the space age. In 1963, New Orleans's Michoud Plant made its first Saturn rocket. In 1969, a Saturn launched *Apollo 11*. That mission landed the first people on the moon.

Louisiana enjoyed rather good times in the late 1970s. Oil prices were high. Taxes from oil and gas provided nearly one-half of the state's money. Much of this wealth was spent on Louisiana's schools and highways. Then, in the 1980s, oil prices dropped. Hundreds of Louisiana wells closed. Thousands of oil and gas workers lost their jobs.

Louisiana's environment has also suffered. Millions of pounds of toxic wastes are released each year. They come from the state's factories and oil plants. Louisiana loses over 50 square miles of wetlands a year. This is partly due to levees (walls) along the Mississippi River. The levees help prevent flooding. But they also keep water from flowing into wetlands. Since 1989, Louisianans have been working to rebuild wetlands.

Business is looking up in Louisiana. In 1992, riverboat and casino gambling became legal in Louisiana. This has brought thousands of jobs and many more tourists. Oil prices are rising again. Gambling and oil money has added millions of tax dollars to the state. Much of the money goes to improve Louisiana's schools. The National Science Foundation also granted Louisiana several million dollars. It is to be used to train math and science teachers. Louisianans know that education is important for the state's future.

Students on a field trip take part in a demonstration at the Aquarium of the Americas, New Orleans.

Overleaf: A costumed woman celebrating Mardi Gras in New Orleans

Louisianans and Their Work

LOUISIANANS AND THEIR WORK

More than 4.2 million people live in Louisiana. Two-thirds of all Louisianans list themselves as white. Most of them have French, English, German, Irish, or Italian backgrounds. Nearly one-third of all Louisianans call themselves black. About 95,000 Louisianans are Hispanic. They come from Spanish-speaking backgrounds. Over 40,000 Louisianans have Asian backgrounds. About 20,000 American Indians live in Louisiana. Many Louisianans are a mix of these groups.

Many Louisianans have French backgrounds and about 20,000 American Indians live in the state.

Louisianans' rich backgrounds helped them develop world-famous foods. The Cajun and Creole recipes are especially popular. Gumbo is a soup or stew. It includes okra, peppers, tomatoes, onions, shrimp, and sausage. Crawfish is in the lobster family. It is another special Louisiana food. Jambalaya is rice mixed with shrimp, sausage, chicken, and seasoning.

Louisiana is well-known for music, too. New Orleans is the "Cradle of Jazz." Black musicians began this music about 100 years ago. They played sad tunes on the way to funerals. But on the way

Left: A trumpet player in New Orleans
Right: Cajun musicians at Vermilionville, in Lafayette

back, they played lively numbers. This music became known as jazz. French-speaking black musicians who live in southwest Louisiana began zydeco. This music mixes French tunes with blues. Cajun musicians play accordions, fiddles, and guitars. Zydeco musicians add washboards.

THEIR WORK

More than 1.6 million Louisianans have jobs. Service work is the leading type of job. Over 400,000 Louisianans are service workers. They include health-care workers and lawyers. They also include hotel workers and others involved in tourism. Louisiana's 20 million yearly visitors make tourism a giant business.

Nearly 380,000 Louisianans sell goods The goods range from oil to groceries. Another 350,000 Louisianans do government work. Many work for the state government in Baton Rouge. Others work for the United States government. About 11,000 people have jobs at the Fort Polk Military Reservation. Nearly 200,000 Louisianans make goods. Chemicals are the state's top product. Louisiana leads the country at making fertilizers. Refined oil, paint, soap, and plastic are other Louisiana-made chemicals. Ships, airplanes, and paper and wooden goods are also made in

Left: A Louisiana paper mill
Right: A shipyard worker welds a boat hull in Amelia

Louisiana. Packaged sugar and candies called pralines are other Louisiana goods.

More than 100,000 Louisianans work in transportation and shipping. Louisiana has the busiest United States port. That is the Port of South Louisiana near Laplace. It handles almost 400 billion pounds of cargo a year. Three other Louisiana ports are among the country's ten busiest. They are the Ports of Baton Rouge, New Orleans, and Plaquemine.

About 50,000 Louisianans farm. Soybeans are the top farm crop. Louisiana is a leading grower of

Harvesting cotton in Boyce

rice, cotton, sugarcane, and sweet potatoes. Strawberries and pecans are other important crops. Louisianans also raise beef and dairy cattle, chickens, and hogs.

Mining employs over 56,000 Louisianans. Oil and natural gas are the top minerals. Louisiana leads the country at mining salt. It ranks second at mining sulfur.

Roughly 16,000 Louisianans fish for a living. The state ranks first at catching shrimp and raising crawfish. Oysters and blue crabs are other important shellfish.

An off-shore oil platform in the Gulf of Mexico, Louisiana

Only Texas has more miners and produces more natural gas. Texas and Alaska are tied as the biggest producers of oil.

Overleaf: Jackson Square, New Orleans

A Louisiana Tour

A LOUISIANA TOUR

Louisiana is a fun state to visit. It offers great food, lively jazz, and colorful festivals. The state's beautiful scenery includes rivers and bayous, hills and prairies. Its lovely cities and towns add a touch of history.

NEW ORLEANS

New Orleans is in southeastern Louisiana. It is a fine place to start a tour. With about 500,000 people, it is Louisiana's biggest city. New Orleans is called the "Crescent City." The French Quarter is a crescent-shaped curve on the Mississippi River. The early French settlers built this part of the city. But fires raced through the French Quarter in 1788 and 1794. It was rebuilt during Spanish rule. French Quarter buildings now have a Spanish style. They are known for their ironwork balconies.

The St. Louis Cathedral towers above the French Quarter. The present cathedral was built in 1794 and remodeled in 1851. It is the country's oldest Catholic cathedral still in use. On either side of the cathedral stand the Cabildo and Presbytere.

A crescent looks like a quarter moon.

Ironwork balconies in the French Quarter

Today, they are part of the Louisiana State Museum. They are good places to learn about Louisiana's history. The Musée Conti Wax Museum has more than 100 wax figures of important Louisianans. Each tells his or her own story by audiotape. The Voodoo Museum is also in the French Quarter. There, visitors can learn about Marie Laveau, the Voodoo Queen.

The French Quarter also has wonderful restaurants. Some of the world's best jazz pours out of French Quarter nightclubs. Preservation Hall is a famous jazz spot. Musicians even perform on the streets in the French Quarter.

An aerial view of New Orleans

Left: A home in the Garden District of New Orleans
Right: The Mardi Gras Parade

Each winter, New Orleans hosts Mardi Gras. It falls on the day before Ash Wednesday. Mardi gras means "fat Tuesday" in French. Mardi Gras is a big party. There are parades, balls, and much to eat. Across town is the Garden District. Americans who arrived after the Louisiana Purchase built homes there. Today, it is still known for its lovely old mansions in garden settings. New Orleans's Aquarium of the Americas draws many visitors. More than 10,000 fish, birds, and reptiles live there. New Orleans also has the world's biggest indoor stadium. That is the Louisiana Superdome. The New Orleans Saints play pro football there.

Jean Lafitte National Historical Park is east of New Orleans at Chalmette. The Battle of New Orleans was fought there. This battle is reenacted on the weekend nearest January 8. The Baratarian unit of the Jean Lafitte National Park is across the river from New Orleans. It has a raised wooden walkway that lets visitors walk through the swamps.

Lake Pontchartrain is north of New Orleans. The world's longest bridge spans the lake. The Second Lake Pontchartrain Causeway is almost 24 miles long. It links Metairie with Covington.

Metairie and Kenner are west of New Orleans. With nearly 150,000 people, Metairie ranks fourth among Louisiana's cities. Metairie's Lafreniere Park has beautiful gardens. It has small lakes for fishing. Seven Oaks is in Kenner. This is a re-created 1795 Louisiana plantation. Kenner is also home to Rivertown, USA. Buildings there have been restored. Children enjoy Rivertown's Louisiana Toy Train Museum.

EASTERN LOUISIANA

Baton Rouge is northwest of New Orleans. It is on the Mississippi River. Long ago, a red pole divided the lands of two Indian groups. The French began a

Above: The Aquarium of the Americas
Below: The Louisiana Toy Train Museum in Kenner

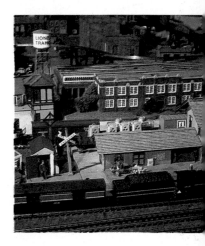

The stained-glass dome of the Old Capitol

Left: The Louisiana State Capitol
Right: The Old Capitol

settlement there in 1719. They named it Baton Rouge. In French that means "red stick."

Today, Baton Rouge is Louisiana's second-largest city. Nearly 220,000 people live there. Baton Rouge is also Louisiana's capital. The Old State Capitol was built in 1849. It looks like a castle. The present state capitol stands thirty-four stories tall. It is the tallest of the country's fifty state capitols. Huey Long had it built in slightly more than a year. He was assassinated in its hallways. His grave is on the capitol's grounds.

Louisiana State University (LSU) is also in Baton Rouge. LSU's Rural Life Museum shows

what plantation life was like. Its buildings include slave cabins and a country church. Baton Rouge's Magnolia Mound dates from the 1790s. The plantation house is built in Creole style. It is raised up on brick posts with an overhanging roof.

East and West Feliciana parishes are north of Baton Rouge. Together, they are called Feliciana Country. St. Francisville is in Feliciana Country. Near the town is Oakley Plantation House. In the 1800s, John James Audubon drew many pictures of birds there. Oakley has been restored to look like it did during Audubon's life.

Farther north is Ferriday. Rock-and-roll stars Jerry Lee Lewis and Mickey Gilley were born there. So was Jimmy Swaggart, a television preacher. The Ferriday Museum opened in 1995 to honor these and other people from Ferriday.

In northeast Louisiana is the Tensas River National Wildlife Refuge. Visitors there can see male wood ducks. These are North America's most colorful ducks. They have green, blue, purple, white, yellow, and red feathers. Hundreds of alligators also crawl about the refuge.

Monroe is to the west on Louisiana's Ouachita River. With about 55,000 people, Monroe is northeast Louisiana's biggest city. Rebecca's Doll

Memorial Tower, Louisiana State University (LSU)

The General Store at LSU's Rural Life Museum

37

*Rebecca's Doll
Museum in Monroe*

Museum is in Monroe. More than 2,000 dolls can be seen there. They were collected by Rebecca Ham. The Louisiana Purchase Gardens and Zoo is another Monroe attraction. It houses one of the world's largest groups of primates. Spider monkeys, lemurs, and gibbons can be seen from boat tours.

NORTHWEST LOUISIANA

West of Monroe is Ruston. It is home to Louisiana Tech University. The Equine Center is there. People learn to race, train, and breed horses at the center. This is the country's most-noted horse program of its kind.

Farther west is Shreveport. Long ago, a 160-mile logjam blocked northwest Louisiana's Red River. Henry Shreve made "snagboats." In the 1830s, he used them to clear the logjam. This helped open northwest Louisiana to settlement. One of Shreve's work camps was named Shreveport. Today, Shreveport is the state's third-biggest city. Almost 200,000 people live there.

Shreveport hosts the Louisiana State Fair in October. The Louisiana State Museum is near the fairgrounds. The museum's dioramas show Louisiana life from prehistoric times to the 1900s.

The American Rose Center is another Shreveport highlight. In sixty different gardens, 20,000 rose bushes grow.

North of Shreveport is Oil City. A large oil field was discovered there in 1906. Today, visitors can learn about oil at the Oil and Historical Museum Complex. Mansfield is south of Shreveport. In 1864, the Battle of Mansfield took place near the town. A 12,000-man Confederate army defeated 25,000 Union troops. Today, the battlefield has a museum showing Civil War weapons and uniforms. To the southeast is Natchitoches. It is on Cane River Lake. Many historic buildings stand in Louisiana's oldest town. Fort St. Jean Baptiste has

Cattle being judged at the Louisiana State Fair in Shreveport

been rebuilt. It looks exactly like the French fort did in 1732.

CENTRAL LOUISIANA

Kisatchie National Forest is Louisiana's only national forest. It is in central Louisiana. People camp and hike in the forest. Fishing and swimming are popular there, too. Alexandria is in the middle of the forest. The Alexandria Museum of Art is in this city. Works by Clementine Hunter and other Louisiana artists are shown there.

Acadian Village, in Lafayette

Fort Polk is to the southwest near Leesville. Soldiers are trained for combat at this army base. The Fort Polk Military Museum has tanks and helicopters. Southwest of Alexandria is Marksville. A great Indian culture grew there 2,000 years ago. Six mounds built by the Tunica still stand. The Tunica-Biloxi Museum is built in the shape of an Indian mound.

To the North is Ville Platte. The Louisiana State Arboretum is nearby. Beech and magnolia trees grow there. Many other Louisiana trees and flowers also grow along the arboretum's trails.

SOUTHERN LOUISIANA

Lake Charles is southwest Louisiana's largest city. More than 70,000 people live there. The lake itself has a white sand beach with palm trees. The Children's Museum is in Lake Charles. Young people love the museum's Kids' Town. They can play in its post office, courtroom, and fire station.

Lafayette is east of Lake Charles. It is called the "Cajun Capital." Many Cajun people live there. Visitors come to enjoy Cajun foods and music. At Lafayette's Acadian Village, visitors can see how Acadians—early Cajuns—lived.

Lafayette is the state's fifth-biggest city.

41

Jungle Gardens, Avery Island

Between Lake Charles and Lafayette are Crowley and Rayne. Crowley hosts the International Rice Festival each fall. Rayne hosts the Frog Festival, also in the fall. Frog-racing and frog-jumping contests are part of the fun.

South of Lafayette is St. Martinville. The Evangeline Oak stands there. It was named after Henry Wadsworth Longfellow's *Evangeline.* This 1847 poem is based on a love story about two Acadians. Their names were Emmeline Labiche and Louis Arceneaux. Longfellow called them Evangeline and Gabriel. On the trip from Canada, they became separated. In St. Martinville, they found each other. They were said to meet at the Evangeline Oak. Louis had married another woman. Emmeline died of a broken heart. Nearby, the Evangeline Statue stands over Emmeline's grave.

A few miles south is New Iberia. This town lies among bayous and swamps. Shadow-on-the-Teche is an 1830s sugar plantation. The main house is red brick with white pillars. Its gardens have huge oaks draped with Spanish moss.

Farther south is Avery Island. This is not a real island. Instead, it is a salt dome. At one time, the McIlhenny family owned the town. Edward Avery McIlhenny built Jungle Gardens around his home.

Tropical plants from around the world grow there. Bird City is in the gardens. Snowy egrets fly about. McIlhenny saved them from being wiped out. The McIlhenny family also developed Tabasco sauce. This is a hot pepper sauce. Tabasco sauce is still made in Avery Island. Visitors can tour the factory.

Houma is not far from Louisiana's southeastern tip. It was founded by Cajuns in 1834. The town has seven bayous and fifty-five bridges. Owls, nutrias, and alligators can be spotted in Houma's bayous. A bayou cruise around Houma is a good way to end a Louisiana tour.

Shadow-on-the-Teche, an 1830s sugar plantation in New Iberia

43

A Gallery of Famous Louisianans

A GALLERY OF FAMOUS LOUISIANANS

Opposite: Louis "Satchmo" Armstrong

Many Louisianans have become great musicians, authors, and athletes. Others have become doctors and lawmakers.
Margaret Gaffney Haughery (1813-1882) was born in Ireland. She lived most of her life in New Orleans. There, Haughery built up a big dairy and bakery. She was called the "Bread Lady." Haughery gave bread and milk to the city's hungry. She also founded homes for the poor. At her death, Haughery's money went to charity. Today, there is a statue of her in New Orleans.

Paul Morphy (1837-1884) was born in New Orleans. In 1859, he became the world's chess champion. One of Morphy's tricks was to play eight games at once—blindfolded.

Adah Isaacs Menken (1835?-1868) was born into a Jewish family. They lived just outside New Orleans. Menken became a famous stage actress. She drew record audiences in the United States and Europe. Menken also wrote poems. A book of her poems was called *Infelicia*.

Clementine Hunter (1886-1988) was born near Cloutierville. She grew up on a plantation near

Adah Isaacs Menken

45

Natchitoches. Hunter began painting in her late fifties. Many were "memory pictures" of black people working. Her thousands of paintings include *African House* and *Cotton Gin*. Hunter painted until her death.

Michael DeBakey was born in Lake Charles in 1908. He became a heart surgeon. Dr. DeBakey saved thousands of heart patients. He made the "assisting heart." This was the first pump to help a sick heart do its work.

George Washington Cable (1844-1925) was born in New Orleans. He was one of Louisiana's first great authors. Cable wrote about Louisiana's Creoles. *Old Creole Days* was one such book. He also wrote about justice for black people. That was long before most white people thought about it.

Kate Chopin (1851-1904) was born in Missouri. After she married, she lived in Louisiana. Chopin wrote about Louisiana Creoles and Cajuns. *Bayou Folk* was one of her books.

Arna Bontemps (1902-1973) was born in Alexandria. He wrote poems and stories about being black. *God Sends Sunday* and *Story of the Negro* are two of them.

Lillian Hellman (1905-1984) was born in New Orleans. She became a great playwright. Hellman

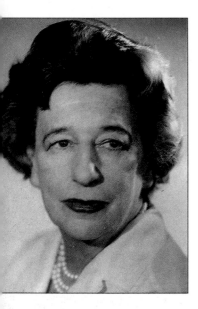

Lillian Hellman

wrote *The Children's Hour* and *Toys in the Attic*. They were about selfishness and evil.

Truman Capote

Truman Capote (1924-1984) was born in New Orleans. He became a writer. Capote won fame at age twenty-four with *Other Voices, Other Rooms*. This strange story is set in a falling-apart Louisiana mansion. His best-known work is *In Cold Blood*. It is about two real-life murderers.

Ernest J. Gaines

Ernest J. Gaines was born in Oscar in 1933. Many of his stories and novels are about black southerners. They are set in the make-believe town of Bayonne, Louisiana. *The Autobiography of Miss Jane Pittman* is his best-known work. It follows a

woman's life from slavery to the civil-rights era (1960s). Gaines's *A Lesson Before Dying* won a 1994 National Book Award.

Anne Rice was born in New Orleans in 1941. She writes strange tales. Many are based in New Orleans. She is best-known for her vampire stories. *Interview with the Vampire* sold 5 million copies. Rice has also written stories about mummies and witches.

Ferdinand La Menthe (Jelly Roll Morton) (1885-1941) was born in New Orleans. He grew up to be one of the world's best jazz musicians. Jelly Roll Morton played the piano and wrote songs. Two of them are "King Porter Stomp" and "Jelly Roll Blues."

Louis "Satchmo" Armstrong (1900-1971) was born in New Orleans. As a boy, he sang on the streets for pennies. Later, he became known as the "World's Greatest Trumpeter." Satchmo also sang. His raspy voice was well known. New Orleans's Louis Armstrong Park was named for him.

Antoine "Fats" Domino was born in New Orleans in 1929. He came from a French-speaking household. He spoke French before he learned English. Fats became a rock-and-roll singer and piano player. His best-known songs are "Blueberry Hill" and "I'm Walkin'."

Jelly Roll Morton

Mahalia Jackson (1911-1972) was also born in New Orleans. She sang in her father's church choir. Jackson became a gospel singer. "He's Got the Whole World in His Hands" was one of her songs.

Mahalia Jackson

Wynton Marsalis

The Marsalises have been called "The First Family of Jazz." They include Ellis Marsalis (born 1934) and six sons. **Branford Marsalis** was born in 1960 and **Wynton Marsalis** was born in 1961. All three were born in New Orleans. Ellis teaches jazz piano. Branford plays jazz and rock saxophone. He led the band on television's "Tonight Show." Wynton is a great trumpet player. He has won eight Grammy Awards.

Left: Mel Ott
Right: Bill Russell

Harry Connick, Jr., was born in New Orleans in 1967. He began studying piano at age six. At age seven, Connick played with adult jazz musicians in the French Quarter. Later, he studied with Ellis Marsalis. In 1990, Connick won a Grammy for best male jazz singer.

Mel Ott (1909-1958) was born in Gretna. He became a great player for the New York Giants. Ott won six home-run crowns. He ended with 511 home runs. In 1951, he was elected to the Baseball Hall of Fame.

Bill Russell was born in Monroe in 1934. He led the University of San Francisco to national basketball titles (1955 and 1956). In 1956, he was on the U.S. basketball team that won an Olympic gold medal. Later, he led the Boston Celtics (1956-1969) to eleven NBA titles. Russell became the Celtic's head coach in 1966. He was the first black person to coach any major U.S. pro team.

Terry Bradshaw was born in Shreveport in 1948. He became a great quarterback. Bradshaw broke every school passing record at Louisiana Tech. Later, he played for the NFL's Pittsburgh Steelers. Bradshaw led the Steelers to four Super Bowl titles (1974, 1975, 1978, and 1979).

Evelyn Ashford was born in Shreveport in 1957. She was a great runner in four Olympics (1976, 1984, 1988, and 1992). Ashford won four Olympic gold medals and two silver medals. Her races were the 100 meter and the 100-meter relay.

Eddie Robinson was born in Jackson in 1919. He became football coach at Louisiana's Grambling State University in 1941. By 1995, 75-year-old Robinson had nearly 400 victories. He was still coaching the Grambling Tigers. Robinson has the most wins of any college football coach ever. More than 200 of his players have become pros.

Evelyn Ashford

51

Michael Hahn (1830-1886) was born in Germany. He came to New Orleans when he was ten. In 1864, Hahn was elected governor of Louisiana. He was one of the country's first Jewish governors. In 1865, he became a U.S. senator from Louisiana. Later, he founded Hahnville near New Orleans.

Edward Douglass White (1845-1921) was born in Lafourche Parish. At age fifteen, he joined the Confederate army and was captured. After his release, White settled in New Orleans. He became a lawyer (1868). Later, White was appointed to the U.S. Supreme Court (1894-1921). He served as chief justice of the country's highest court from 1910 to 1921.

Hale Boggs (1914-1972) was born in Mississippi. He served Louisiana in the U.S. House of Representatives (1941-1943 and 1947-1972). In 1972, he died in an airplane crash. **Lindy Boggs**, his wife, was elected to fill his seat (1972-1991). Lindy was born in Pointe Coupee Parish in 1916. Both Hale and Lindy worked for the rights of black people.

Cleo Fields was born in Baton Rouge in 1962. In 1986, Fields became the youngest state senator in Louisiana history. He then was elected to the

U.S. House of Representatives (1992). Fields *Hale Boggs* became the youngest member of Congress.

The birthplace of Cleo Fields, Louis Armstrong, Lillian Hellman, and Clementine Hunter . . .

Home, too, of Hale Boggs, Michael Hahn, Margaret Gaffney Haughery, and John James Audubon . . .

First in the country at producing salt, shrimp, and crawfish . . .

The birthplace of jazz and the land of gumbo and jambalaya . . .

This is the Pelican State—Louisiana!

Did You Know?

The longest railroad bridge in the United States is the Huey P. Long Bridge. Its span is 4.4 miles long across the Mississippi River outside New Orleans.

The word *alligator* comes from *el lagarto*, which means "the lizard" in Spanish. Spanish explorers named this animal. Louisiana wetlands are now home to about 500,000 alligators.

More than 1 million people attend Mardi Gras each year in New Orleans.

Avery Island sits atop a salt dome. During the Civil War, the island's salt was mined for the Confederate army.

Tangipahoa, northeast of Baton Rouge, was the first United States town founded by a woman. "Granny" Rhoda Mixon began it in 1806.

Southern Louisiana's Atchafalaya Basin is one of the country's largest wetlands. It is home to more than 5 million ducks and geese.

Louisiana produces about 60 million pounds of crawfish a year. They are served in soups, stews, gumbo, and jambalaya.

Cajun French, once spoken commonly in Louisiana's Cajun Country, now has to be taught to young people in area schools.

Louisiana's West Feliciana Parish has the country's largest bald cypress. This 83-foot-tall tree has a trunk that is almost 54 feet around. Louisiana's St. Tammany Parish has the country's biggest live oak. It is 55 feet tall and 36.7 feet around.

The St. Charles line in New Orleans is part of the country's oldest streetcar line. Service began in 1835. The Wedding Cake House is one of the landmarks it passes.

In the early New Orleans cemeteries, the graves were built above the ground so flooding wouldn't wash them away. Enclosed by iron fences, these "cities of the dead" look like little towns with small, white stone houses.

Waterproof is in northeast Louisiana. The town was given that name for good luck after it was moved several times due to floods. Nearby Frogmore reportedly got its name because so many frogs lived there.

In 1948, Russell Long became the first person to win a U.S. Senate seat held earlier by both parents. His father, Huey Long, and his mother, Rose McConnell Long, had also held the seat.

Louisiana Information

State flag

Magnolia blossom

Catahoula leopard dog

Area: 47,752 square miles (the thirty-first-biggest state)

Greatest Distance North to South: 283 miles

Greatest Distance East to West: 315 miles

Borders: Mississippi to the east; Arkansas to the north; Texas to the west; the Gulf of Mexico to the south and east

Highest Point: Driskill Mountain, 535 feet above sea level

Lowest Point: New Orleans, 5 feet below sea level

Hottest Recorded Temperature: 114° F. (at Plain Dealing, on August 10, 1936)

Coldest Recorded Temperature: -16° F. (at Minden, on February 13, 1899)

Statehood: The eighteenth state, on April 30, 1812

Origin of Name: French explorer René-Robert Cavelier, Sieur de La Salle, named Louisiana for King Louis XIV of France

Capital: Baton Rouge (permanently since 1882)

Previous Capitals: New Orleans (1812-1830, 1831-1849, 1862-1882), Donaldsonville (1830-1831), and Baton Rouge (1849-1862)

Parishes (called counties in other states): 64

United States Representatives: 7 (as of 1992)

State Senators: 39

State Representatives: 105

State Songs: "Give Me Louisiana," by Doralice Fontane; "You Are My Sunshine," by Jimmy H. Davis and Charles Mitchell

State Motto: "Union, Justice, and Confidence"

Nicknames: "Pelican State," "Bayou State," "Creole State," "Sportsman's Paradise," "Sugar State"

State Seal: Adopted in 1902   **State Flag:** Adopted in 1912

State Flower: Magnolia   **State Tree:** Bald cypress

State Bird: Brown pelican   **State Dog:** Catahoula leopard dog

State Insect: Honeybee   **State Fossil:** Petrified palmwood

State Gemstone: Agate   **State Colors:** Gold, white, and blue

Some Rivers: Mississippi, Red, Black, Calcasieu, Sabine, Ouachita, Atchafalaya, Pearl

Some Lakes: Lake Pontchartrain, Catahoula, Grand, White, Salvador

Some Bayous: Boeuf, Bonne Idee, Nezpique, Teche, Lafourche

Some Islands: Marsh, Grand Isle, Timbalier, Chandeleur, Breton

Wildlife: Alligators, nutrias, deer, bears, bobcats, raccoons, otters, rabbits, foxes, wild hogs, opossums, muskrats, mink, skunks, gophers, tortoises, snapping turtles, sea turtles, dolphins, pelicans, ducks, geese, doves, egrets, woodpeckers, swans, herons, eagles, cranes, owls, many other kinds of birds, water moccasins, and other snakes

Farm Products: Soybeans, rice, cotton, sugarcane, corn, pecans, strawberries, sweet potatoes, beef and dairy cattle, milk, chickens, eggs, hogs

Manufactured Products: Fertilizers, medicines, paint, plastics, refined oil, ships, truck trailers, aircraft, lumber, paper and wooden goods, packaged sugar, coffee, soft drinks, clothing, glass

Mining Products: Oil, natural gas, salt, sulfur, sand and gravel, coal

Fishing Products: Shrimp, crawfish, oysters, blue crabs, menhaden

Population: 4,219,973, twenty-first among the states (1990 U.S. Census Bureau figures)

Major Cities (1990 Census):

New Orleans	496,938	Kenner	72,033
Baton Rouge	219,531	Lake Charles	70,580
Shreveport	198,525	Monroe	54,909
Metairie	149,428	Bossier City	52,721
Lafayette	94,440	Alexandria	49,188

Bald cypress

Brown pelican

LOUISIANA HISTORY

Jean Baptiste Le Moyne founded New Orleans.

About 10,000 B.C.—The first people reach Louisiana

1541—Hernando De Soto leads Spaniards into Louisiana

1682—René-Robert Cavelier, Sieur de La Salle, reaches the mouth of the Mississippi River, claims all land drained by the river for France, and names the land Louisiana

1714—Natchitoches, today Louisiana's oldest town, is begun

1718—Jean Baptiste Le Moyne begins New Orleans

1722—New Orleans becomes French Louisiana's capital

1760s-1790s—About 4,000 French settlers, known as Acadians, arrive from Canada

1762—France gives Louisiana to Spain in a secret treaty

1788—Fire destroys most of New Orleans

1794—Louisiana's first newspaper, *Le Moniteur de la Louisiana (Louisiana Monitor)*, is published in New Orleans

1800—Spain returns Louisiana to France

1803—The United States buys French Louisiana, which includes New Orleans and Louisiana west of the Mississippi, as well as all or part of fourteen other states

1810—Louisiana east of the Mississippi River is claimed by the United States from Spain

1812—Louisiana becomes the eighteenth state on April 30

1815—Andrew Jackson wins the Battle of New Orleans

1819—The United States and Spain sign a treaty making land east of the Sabine River part of Louisiana

1861—Louisiana secedes from the United States on January 26

1861-65—Louisiana provides about 56,000 troops for the Confederacy during the Civil War

1865—Southern slaves are freed by the Union (Northern) victory; Louisiana comes under U.S. military control

1868—Louisiana is readmitted to the United States on June 25

1877—U.S. troops leave Louisiana

1882—Baton Rouge becomes Louisiana's capital

1898—The vote is taken away from Louisiana's black residents

1901—Oil is found in Louisiana

1916—Natural gas is found in the state

1917-18—Louisiana provides about 75,000 troops to help win World War I

1928—Huey Long becomes Louisiana's governor

1929-39—The Great Depression hurts Louisiana and the rest of the nation

1935—Huey Long is murdered in Louisiana's state capitol

1941-45—After the United States enters World War II, nearly 300,000 Louisiana men and women serve

1956—The Second Lake Pontchartrain Causeway, the world's longest over-water highway bridge, opens

1957—Hurricane Audrey kills over 350 people in Louisiana

1973—Lindy Boggs becomes the first woman from Louisiana in the U.S. House of Representatives

1975—The Louisiana Superdome, the world's biggest indoor stadium, is completed in New Orleans

1977—Ernest N. Morial is elected New Orleans's first black mayor

1984—New Orleans hosts the Louisiana World Exposition, a world's fair

1990—Louisiana's population is 4,219,973

1991—Edwin Edwards wins his fourth term as Louisiana's governor; Melinda Schwegmann is elected as Louisiana's first woman lieutenant governor

1995—Severe floods destroy thousands of Louisiana homes and kill at least six people

A mother kisses her son goodbye before he goes overseas during World War I.

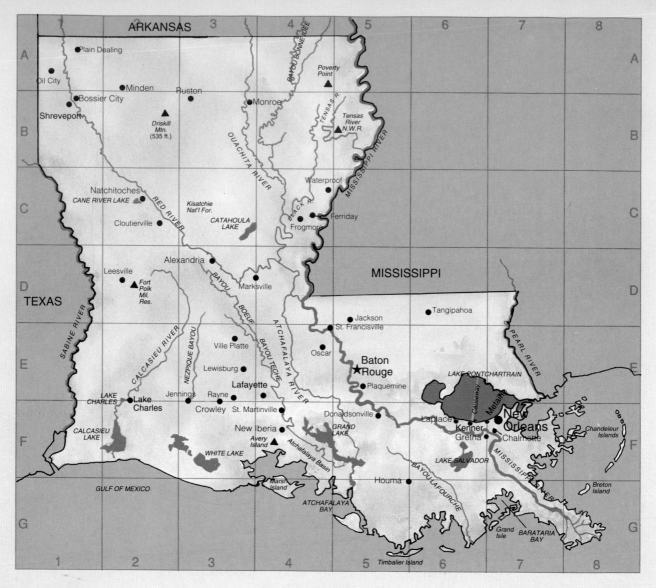

MAP KEY

GLOSSARY

ancient: Relating to a time or people of long ago

arboretum: A place where trees and other plants are grown for people to study and enjoy

bayou: Slow-moving, often marshy water that is an inlet or outlet for a lake or a river

billion: A thousand million (1,000,000,000)

capital: The city that is the seat of government

capitol: The building in which the government meets

climate: The typical weather of a region

descendant: A person who comes after other people in a family, such as a child, grandchild, or great-grandchild

explorer: A person who visits and studies unknown lands

fossil: The remains of an animal or plant that lived long ago

gospel music: Religious music with elements of folk music and blues

gumbo: A soup or stew typically containing seafood and vegetables

hurricane: A strong windstorm that forms over the ocean and does great damage if it reaches land

industry: A business activity that requires many people and much equipment

irrigation: The watering of land through artificial methods

jazz: A lively music that was born in New Orleans

levee: The wall built to keep a river from flooding

million: A thousand thousand (1,000,000)

parish: Louisiana's political unit that is similar to a county in the other states

plains: Generally flat lands

plantation: A very large farm, usually using slave labor

population: The number of people in a place

secede: To withdraw from or leave

segregation: The process of keeping people of different races apart

sharecropper: A person who farms on another person's land and who must give a share of the farm crops to the landowner

slavery: A practice in which one group of people own people from another group

swamp: A marshy wetland where trees grow and many kinds of animals live

tenant farmer: A person who rents farmland from a landowner

tourism: The business of providing such services as food and lodging for visitors

PICTURE ACKNOWLEDGMENTS

Front cover, ©H. Abernathy/**H Armstrong Roberts**; 1, ©**Philip Gould**; 2, **Tom Dunnington**; 3, ©Bob Thomason/**Tony Stone Images, Inc.**; 4-5, **Tom Dunnington**; 6-7, ©**Thomas Ritter**; 8, ©**Thomas Ritter**; 9 (left), ©**Tom Till**; 9 (right), **Courtesy of Hammond Incorporated, Maplewood, New Jersey**; 10 (left), ©Jim Battles/**Dembinsky Photo Assoc.**; 10 (right), ©Mary A. Root/**Root Resources**; 11, ©Christopher Harris/**SuperStock**; 12, **The Historic New Orleans Collection**, accession no. 1979.325.2944; 13, ©Garry D. McMichael/**Root Resources**; 14, **The Historic New Orleans Collection**, accession no. 1970.1; 15, ©**David J. Forbert**; 17, **North Wind Picture Archives**, color lithograph; 18 (top), **The Bettmann Archive**; 18 (bottom), **Stock Montage, Inc.**; 19, **The Bettmann Archive**; 20, **UPI/Bettmann**; 21, **AP/Wide World Photos**; 23, ©Jim Schwabel/**N E Stock Photo**; 24, ©Donna Carroll/**Travel Stock**; 25 (top), ©**Carolyn Thornton**; 25 (bottom), ©**Thomas Ritter**; 26 (left), ©Bob Krist/**Tony Stone Images, Inc.**; 26 (right), ©W. Bertch/**H. Armstrong Roberts**; 27 (left), ©Ron Sherman/**Tony Stone Images, Inc.**; 27 (right), ©Buddy Mays/**Travel Stock**; 28, ©Garry D. McMichael/**Root Resources**; 29, ©**Cameramann International, Ltd.**; 30-31, ©Scott Berner/**mga/Photri**; 32, ©David M. Doody/**Tom Stack & Associates**; 33, ©Manfred Gottschalk/**Tom Stack & Associates**; 34 (left), ©**David J. Forbert**; 34 (right), ©Jim Pickerell/**Tony Stone Images, Inc.**; 35 (top), ©Scott Berner/**Photri, Inc.**; 35 (bottom), ©**David J. Forbert**; 36 (top), ©**Carolyn Thornton**; 36 (bottom left), ©John Elk/**Tony Stone Images, Inc.**; 36 (bottom right), ©James Blank/**Root Resources**; 37 (top), ©**Cameramann International, Ltd.**; 37 (bottom), ©**Joan Dunlop**; 38, ©**David J. Forbert**; 39, ©**Philip Gould**; 40, ©R. Krubner/**H. Armstrong Roberts**; 42, ©**David J. Forbert**; 43, ©Jim Schwabel/**N E Stock Photo**; 44, **AP/Wide World Photos**; 45, **The Bettmann Archive**; 46, **AP/Wide World Photos**; 47 (top), **UPI/Bettmann**; 47 (bottom), **AP/Wide World Photos**; 48, **The Bettmann Archive**; 49 (top), **UPI/Bettmann**; 49 (bottom), **Wide World Photos, Inc.**; 50 (both pictures), **UPI/Bettmann**; 51, **AP/Wide World Photos**; 53, **Bettmann**; 54-55 (top), ©Les Riess/**Photri, Inc.**; 54 (bottom), ©Mark J. Thomas/**Dembinsky Photo Assoc.**; 55, **The Historic New Orleans Collection**, accession no. 1974.25.6.629; 56 (top), **Courtesy Flag Research Center, Winchester, Massachusetts 01890**; 56 (middle), ©Carol Christensen/**N E Stock Photo**; 56 (bottom), ©**R. Williamson**; 57 (top), ©**Jerry Hennen**; 57 (bottom), ©Barbara Gerlach/**Dembinsky Photo Assoc.**; 58, **The Historic News Orleans Collection**, accession no. 1991.34.7; 59, **AP/Wide World Photos**; 60, **Tom Dunnington**; back cover, ©Lewis H.Ellsworth/**Photri, Inc.**

INDEX

Page numbers in boldface type indicate illustrations.

ABOUT THE AUTHORS

Dennis and Judith Fradin have coauthored several books in the From Sea to Shining Sea series. The Fradins both graduated from Northwestern University in 1967. Dennis has been a professional writer for twenty years, and has published 150 books. His works for Childrens Press include the Young People's Stories of Our States series, the Disaster! series, and the Thirteen Colonies series. Judith earned her M.A. in literature from Northwestern University and taught high-school and college English for many years. The Fradins, who are the parents of Anthony, Diana, and Michael, live in Evanston, Illinois.